THE WINE-DARK HOUSE

By
Rustin Larson

BLUE LIGHT PRESS ◆ 1ST WORLD PUBLISHING

1st WORLD
PUBLISHING

SAN FRANCISCO ◆ FAIRFIELD ◆ DELHI

THE WINE-DARK HOUSE

Copyright ©2009 by Rustin Larson

All rights reserved. Printed in the United States of America. No part of this book may be used or reproduced in any manner whatsoever without written permission except in the case of brief quotations embodied in critical articles and reviews. For information contact:

1ST WORLD LIBRARY
106 South Court Street
Fairfield, Iowa 52556
www.1stworldpublishing.com

BLUE LIGHT PRESS
1563 45th Avenue
San Francisco, California, 94122

AUTHOR PHOTO
Kate Larson

BOOK DESIGN
Melanie Gendron
www.melaniegendron.com

COVER ART
"Floral" by Nort

"A True Account of Talking to the Sun at Fire Island",
from THE COLLECTED POEMS OF FRANK O'HARA
by Frank O'Hara, edited by Donald Allen, copyright c 1971 by Maureen
Granville-Smith, Administratrix of the Estate of Frank O'Hara. Used by
permission of Alfred A. Knopf, a division of Random House, Inc.

FIRST EDITION

LCCN: 2009923469

ISBN: 978-1-4218-9077-7

CONTENTS

Part One

Part Two

Part Three

Part Four

About the Author

ACKNOWLEDGMENTS

Gratitude is expressed to the editors of the following publications where some of these poems, sometimes in different versions, first appeared:

The Amherst Review "Viva La Sestina"
Apocalypse "Walking with William Blake Under the Trees at Lake Darling"
Boundary 2 "At the Break of Day on My Wooden Porch"
Bryant Literary Review "The Gerbils," "Comparison/Contrast"
Calliope "Dear Roger," "The Emperor's Tapestry," "Improbability's Best Friend, Rejection," "Seascape at Saintes-Maries-De-La-Mer"
Carnelian "On the Destruction of Barhydt Chapel"
Crying Sky "Adjunct," "Blue Notes"
Defined Providence "The Angel," "The Barbecue," "Trying to Survive Death's Little Weather," "The Wine-Dark House"
Illya's Honey "The Dingleberry Tree" (which appeared as "Giant Night Hides in the Storyteller's Pupils"), "Moveable Feast"
The Iowa Source "I Have a New Brain"
Lilies and Cannonballs "Poem"
Loonfeather "The Electric Moon," "1969"
The MacGuffin "Ophelia Drowning," "Robespierre is Dead"
Margie "Sign of the Times," "A Useful Member of Society"
The Mid-America Poetry Review "Copper Dislocation"
Panoply "Both Halves Together"
Passages North "Loving the Good Driver," "The Mosquito," "Poem Without Eyelids"
Pavement "Father"
Phantasmagoria "Winter Window"
Poem "Teacher"
Poetry East "The Invalid," "The Lamp," "Where It Happens"
Rhino "Night and Spinach"

Saranac Review "Character & Setting," "The New Painting"
The South Carolina Review "An Ordinary Drinking Glass"
Tar River Poetry "Baker's"
Water-Stone Review the epigraph for part 4, which appeared as a poem titled "Teacher"
"The Des Moines Rising at Bentonsport" appeared in the anthology *Forty Days and Forty Nights* (Iowa Arts Council, 1993).
"From Their Orbit in the High Dark" appeared in the chapbook *Lord of the Apes* (Conestoga Zen Press, 2001).

PART ONE

"Sun, don't go!" I was awake
at last. "No, go I must, they're calling
me."
    "Who are they?"
                      Rising he said "Some
day you'll know. They're calling to you
too." Darkly he rose, and then I slept.

                        —Frank O'Hara

BAKER'S

doesn't exist now. That corner. The way
the road dipped down into a cavern
of overhang, branches of soft maple.
The blue summer shade, the white glare of Route 5

at the mouth of July and August.
'66, the sweet alcohol
of bay rum splashed on razored jowls, the buzz
clippers giving Duke and Rayball butches.

Buck fifty folded into
a package in my fist, I'd wait, feel the cool rails
of the chair, cold leather near the drip
drip hum of the air conditioner, the TV

mounted on the wall, the Match Game, my turn
on the booster, the tightening
of the disposable collar, the striped apron
covering my bare knees, tennis shoes. Baker

would take a crackle off his Pall Mall, breathe
a jet of smoke as he trimmed. A head
he surely dreamed would someday be sent home
in a blue silk box from Asia. I stared at

        E
     R   K
   '   A
S   B

2

curved in a pagoda, the large-pane frown
projected on the parking lot and gush of semis
in the shimmering heat. My hair
cool, short; time ran

into the cartoon show. A teenage boy waited,
thumbed through the jungle green and Incredible Hulk.

CHARACTER & SETTING

Scratches some
Student had etched
With the end of a compass, Georgetown,

You mistakenly thought
The world had a place of honor
For poets. You were

Just a boy, have mercy on you, you
Didn't understand, had a wife
Who would be pregnant soon, thought

You could find somehow a job where
They would appreciate your similes—
It was fall, but that didn't matter.

The magnolias magnificently
Replaced their lives—you wrote about
Flowers—their

Shapes & femininity
& didn't understand you
Had to work for money—thought

There were grants for you—god forgive
You—fifteen years thought
Of nothing else—thought Mozart

Was an apartment—thought Bach
Was food on the table—you hid
In libraries, thinking the damaged

4

Surface of a table was art.

An Indian restaurant on Sunday,

Wisconsin Avenue;
Curried cauliflower,

Samosas & pakoras, you
Dipped the appetizers in weird green
Sauce that smacked of mint,

Sipped the strange tea of floating
Cardamom, thought every
Syllable was a treasure—a gold

Witnessed into your hand.
The traffic
Was slow—it was

A holiday of balled-up newspaper—the city burned
A light bulb for every
Gesture. It was overcast. You yearned

For news from home. Your wife was

Beautiful in plum—the plum scarf
& blouse. Overcast, it
Wanted to rain & you had a few words

For it.
But they weren't enough.
The baby was surely coming as

The lights of cars
Illuminated the first few drops
Of rain & Krishna sat with women

On some green stretch of grass,
Strand of flowers for a necktie
&

Gold for ink,
Watching
That slow Sunday

In Georgetown,
September 22nd , the fog

Billowing off the river,
Grasping the bridge
In a soft fist.

ON THE DESTRUCTION OF BARHYDT CHAPEL

The sky echoing. Wordsworth's Prelude. My life.
I've never dreamed a darker empty stage.
"I am off in search," Wordsworth told his wife,
"of a vision." My mind's been lost for ages
on boughs of sound. A campus with
a chapel I translated into Tintern.
It was the place I got my first breath:
Romantics, a lit major, a dry urn,
the clouds echoing, lines composed, my own life.
They'll tear the place down to a month of stones—
in sunflower and yarrow and loosestrife—
they'll take the months and pile them into zones,
chunked-up lots, memory: a church not lost
to literature and youth, its Pentecost.

WINTER WINDOW

You can make out this silence. Shadow-room:
two or three potted plants on a rough desk.
A window thinking two tough frosted blooms

of leaded glass, light pulsating a brisk
snow cover on hills, fields, dried milkweed,
a suffocating New Hampshire white.

He mixes Sanka in an old jelly jar
with a shot of hot water from his sink--
an old man, most of his poetry far

behind-- he sips tepid coffee. Snow. Ink.
A final scripting surface. Inscription.
Though dark inside, vines still dream a wild light.

Goodbye, room; I have filled you like a smoke,
he says, he speaks, speaking, has spoken, spoke.

THE DINGLEBERRY TREE

When the dingleberry tree rises
    tall into the dusky blue
        its white bark famous for miles
with each dingleberry singing its own sway
    in the critical wind   each berry
        the globed earring of a luscious angel
prim with the powder of clouds
    and clothed by gowns of drifting pollen
        and mists of ocean perfume

the solid wind pours through
    the windows poorly made
        the piano quiet for an evening
the tea kettle cold
    the new metal of the moon
        black with beginning

    in the elephant woods
        dingleberry trees grow
protected by the ivory of the dead

        many trains   thunder
past the hobo village
    the poor hungry fires
    of coffee and   flesh

        the wind   divided
      by the spire of the tabernacle of nothing
      the jewels of her kiss with which I wash
              my sorrow for bed   her watery tongue
over the holy fires of my thirst

      water the dingleberry
for the flash of the soul's sun upon the sea
      in the night of my morning
              my dream's awakening eye

MOVEABLE FEAST

The man is Italian in the heart of his coffee.
      His tears are diluted with cream.
            And when the cypress shadows

his doorstep, he knows it is time
      to wander and forget.
            The mountain has many unfortunate things

for him and the small hills
      down which not one green olive will roll.
            He had his chances in the desire

of something long and rambling.
      The train that is always late
            is on time today.

It glides into the station with an orgasm
      of steam. Many beautiful women
            step from the observation car.

Their hats are draped in mosquito netting;
      a blue fly knocks against the pane
            in the dim waiting room.

A cherry coal gleams
      in the pipe
            of the abortionist.

His wife has terminated
      their marriage which is almost
            an impossibility in this country

of hills yawning in the shade
       of a passing cloud.
              There will be no rain today.

A little girl
       untwists the foil
              of a chocolate:

the train clanks into motion.
       He believes in his shoes
              and his one dirty suit.

He's been smoking
       for some time now
              to stave off the hunger.

The train gains momentum, speeds
       over a very flat landscape—wheat fields--
              and never stops.

BLUE NOTES

Sound of a trumpet like a little blue night,

like a mist. Let my eyes grow dark

with the sky, the silence resting

in the branches.   Let me be

the rain that feeds the lawn,

that tins the rooftops and glazes the stones.

Pioneer's bearded and primitive sleep,

noises that cloud my mind like sawdust,

cup of dreams, rainbows, and soft folding orchids,

the sun hit you in a low polished light and vanished.

The scent of worms and severed roots,

the bare branches whisper among themselves,

some invisible season resting on them.

There is no laughter inside this rock.

Mary in heaven, Mary in the bones

of a woman, I've slept until blackness

has cherished everything, the night resonating

with a dog's bark some distance away,

a flat dirt pen, the crack of summer thunder,

the valley turning on its side.

ADJUNCT

In my empty classroom,
    I look out the window.
        The snow falls. It's cliché

And real. My view threads through the branches
    Of a bare crabapple tree and through licorice
        Utility wires to the whitening cake

Of the funeral home's parking lot. A truck's brakes
    Honk to a stop. Today, my daughters are in
        Their own classrooms with the vibrancy

Of crayons and the vaguely watery smell
    Of Manila paper... I feel
        The cold blond desktops they rest their arms upon,

Want to wrap myself in a blanket and close my eyes.
    I have another class to teach in five minutes.
        In the spring, I want to wander some; I

Want to walk up a hill. It's quiet now,
    And I hope it snows all day.

At times, I would like to be one of my own children,
    Want the world to be a gift to me. And some
        Times I take it. And some times it is.

A cart vendor could make his way through
    The blowing snow and stop near an alley
        And unwrap handfuls of flame

And take in $1.50 for each combusting
        Apple or grapefruit or plum.
                I do believe in that fire—

Like the torch in the thorny heart
        Jesus revealed as he hovered
                On the wall of my grandmother's

Cottage. Her cottage was sheathed in ice and snow.
        I was eight years old. I felt so alone I
                Felt any story could be mine. My grand-

Mother and I would watch black and white
        Movies at night. I could feel the uniform
                Of the French foreign legion on my skin.

She would give me 50 cents in the morning
        To travel through the snow to French's store
                To buy cream for my thawing raspberries.

The blown ice felt like needles on my face.
        The flame was somewhere deep inside
                My parka. It flickered and rose.

My heart was not crowned by so many thorns—
        Just a few. I don't know where my mother
                Was, nor my father. My crowned

Heart was the foreground of a huge
        Field in the earliness of spring—no
                Flowers but a yellowness of not yet

Revived grasses. There was one robin
  Hopping across the field, and
    It was not singing. The sky was a huge

Gray eiderdown; the sun, one sustained
  Soft note behind.

POEM

I had no idea I had no idea I forgot where
ideas came from I had no idea I was
afraid of the ideas I was failing to have
I was afraid of my failure to have ideas
I had no idea I was afraid of ideas although
the ideas I was having of having no
ideas were making me afraid I had no
idea how afraid until I booked my thoughts
in a diary and saw first-hand both
the fear and the ideas that were and
were not there I had no idea I forgot
where the ideas had come from I had
no thoughts I had no ideas I had
no thoughts about the ideas I had I
had no ideas about the thoughts and
in this silence in this silence in
this silence were hands and feet
hands and feet waiting and hands
folded into a calm and feet
cadencing an anxiety in a world
with no ideas no thoughts no
major disruptions the buildings
still standing no dust no mortar
no brick no wire no avalanche the buildings
still standing no ideas no thought
no ideas no failure

THE GERBILS

Happily busy in the middle of the night,
Destroying their cardboard tube. To sleep
They make a hurricane of straw and declare
This is the middle of us—enough
Already. And their greatest achievement
Is destruction. I love these animals.
Happy enough with their cubes
Of unhappiness for dinner and beads
Of water from the metal tube. Cal
Spins the luck of his wheel and Reb
Files a song on the bars of their cage.
And Wil stuffs his nose in his haystack
And dreams of stuffing his nose in hay,
All while I worry my life away.

WHERE IT HAPPENS

Take a bench.
  It's movable.
    Point it toward the river.

Note the sandbar.
  The eagle circling.
    Next to your heart.

See the village across
  where they fired pottery
    long ago.

The geese waddle
  up the banks.
    You've been here before.

The foundation walls
  of the mill,
    the arches

where its doors once stood,
  the dormant rose garden
    where millers surely labored once

in mote-filled light.
  You are amazed now
    in mild December,

orphaned,
      hungry,
            with a hand in full seed.

And your eyes change
      the light into shadow,
            and the shadow into light.

It's OK. It's OK.
      You're going to be
            all right.

COPPER DISLOCATION

In it the wilderness.
       Say the seasons
              have brought forth my hand

upon a can of salmon
       and the lake water's
              breakfast of light.

I rev the engine
       and the water becomes
              a morning whiskey

mouthwash–
       the sun a newspaper
              of blindness–all I want to know.

Talked to Woody by the fire–
       he sang that lullaby
              to the rails and boxcars.

And then a loon howled
       and Woody smiled like he knew
              that loneliness in such a shadow.

When the whistle announced
       twenty long miles run
              I made eggs and bacon.

We sopped up the grease
       with white bread and chewed.
              And thought a while.

COMPARISON/CONTRAST

His elegy is good, but his elegy is not
Good. His whisper tends to shrink
The leaves, but his whisper is acrid
And extends into a ghost of flame.
His pain eats a Danish on the way
To work on 5th and then dies, but his pain leans
On an empty Steinway on the cold
Dark stage of the civic center and doesn't die. His
Multiplication feeds a few children
In the slums of Brazil, but his
Multiplication gorges on a sunset
Of bay red water and a soft
Wind. His drink makes him sleepy
And makes him think much, but
His drink makes him foolish and
Makes him walk forever.

PART TWO

THE UPPER IOWA RIVER CURVED THROUGH AN OPEN VALLEY FLANKED BY WOODED HILLSIDES

There wasn't much else in this cowless pasture,
1909: an early morning
mist hiding distant bluffs—
a landscape devoid of anything
but suggestions of itself
as memory (that not any one's
but a silver tint developed
in a pleat of seconds passed
continuously on the same spot)

unnoticed except by the casual photographer,
who was, herself, brushing off
corn muffin from the folds of her dress—
breakfasting with young Mr. Lex,
the pale minister's son from Luther
College, and then she stood, perhaps
saying, "Look, Horton, how those
ash breathe the mist..." snapping
the picture with the black box. Even after

they had married and become annoyed
with each other—he a pastor
of a church wounded near the cold
river, she a mistress of white
embroidery—the photograph shimmered
on the mantel like a specimen brain—
a sacred memory of memory—
a velocity quite still and fatal
as the last smile or handshake
or delicate offering of cranberry puff.

POEM WITHOUT EYELIDS

I wake up in the middle of the night, starving.
The refrigerator throbs and drones like a molecular transporter
beaming Captain Snarg down to the planet of sterile
wingback chairs. My stomach groans and the night is full
of elegant monsters reborn with an aesthetic for Mozart
and Brahms blown through the hollowed bones
of Hezekiah Corpseface, railroad magnate of the 1860's
and gracious funder of the slaughter at Shiloh.
So I pour myself a bowl of raisin bran, some generic facsimile,
my teeth admiring the brittleness of the large
flakes, my neck paining from the labor
of my jaws, and I look out the window to see if any of my neighbors
are awake—the cold blue stare from the lights
of the James' Christmas tree. I am alone
with a sliver of glass in my foot—remnant of the tumbler
my wife smashed to the agony of the dirty kitchen floor
days ago. I am awake perhaps only with the 98-year-old
woman who lives a block away having the night nurse feed
another cassette noir to the video machine waiting for death
to sprawl on Pier 5, the light showering on the body
from a lone streetlamp under which the hard-boiled dick
embraced Veronica Lake's cascade of hair moments ago.

I suppose I will try to fall asleep again, slide in under
the draft of the window and pull the comforter over me
like a lawn and try not to feel spring. Although near Christmas,
I can feel bulbs of fatigue planted in my belly, fertilized
by my bad choices in clothes and language. And I suppose
the day is nearing I'll have to face flowers with names,
bend down and kiss the little lips of crocuses, and have them
figure so prominently in a future bout of insomnia on the Wyoming range

or in the Arizona desert where slit-eyed women from the Pleiades
are pinning plastic roses to the saguaros, whispering the time
is now for which all men have been waiting, bowels of digested
raisin bran in their gracefully thin hands, offering, offering,
the doors of the molecular transporter open brightly like a clear day
at Loch Ness, humming like bagpipes lodged in the asshole of a
plesiosaur.

THE MOSQUITO

Look at the dock all twisted and abandoned
as if the most important thought was water
insisting everything return to the primal poverty,
the intention of heaven. I think of the intoxication
of the earth itself, its rampant green thoughts injecting
joy in me, as a virus, a disease, an erasure, a problem
given me in starting over. I sit here
and my hands dent the face
of the planet with pyramids. Like the dog

waiting to come in out of the rain,
that stopped dog which could be the rain itself,
the rain waiting to stop, I could be an hour ticking
away, a motive questioning its worth,
though the only motive worth questioning has already gotten me
born. As my hands change into the petals of orchids, why not
try to attract some symbiotic insect? Why not be irresistible
to the point of disappearing? Looking
at the crumbling dock, I can say
that all this may not be worth much, but
it's me saying it, feeling important. I may not be

an expert on emotion, but look at those
silver-leaved maples over there, the ones with women's
faces. I have every responsibility to be in love
with them, though their profiles are beautiful and looking away.
As it rains, probably I'll say nothing but feel
like I treated them to supper, me standing here in their green
indifference: If I made them happy, what difference
would it make?

There's a mosquito in my heart and I'm humming.
You'd think it would have found the meaning of excess, but
it wants out. It would like to be delicate again.
As it is, I think it feels like a character
from a forgotten alphabet, suspended
in the red weight of neglect.

IN THE HERB GARDEN

Picking the ones that heal, the ones to eat,
to brew, to hang for fragrance, I walk
with my new wife, her moist palm
in mine. The herbs fountain
from the ground: sunlovers,
shadelovers, those finding it hard.
Unnerved by the stranger we married,
we search for the right plant to solve us.
I discover one, gold and dried, hanging
from the ceiling of the herb cottage.
We should brew this as tea, bathe in it:
its essences clearing our blood,
synchronizing heartbeats, and breath.
She uncovers a cluster of green, holds it
like a bride's bouquet, saying we should both
hold on until we trust its fragility
in the different seasons: her
early spring, my autumn.

FLOATERS
—after Roger Weingarten

Sometimes the debris
of my colliding thoughts I see projected
in the sky resembles giant amoebae
grouping to strangle the sun
in one jelly ring.
Sometimes it floats, perfectly round,
translucent planets bubbling closer,
elusive as bees, gathering the air I breathe
with my sparsely populated vocabulary
into the poems I feel
so damned good about. One Sunday,
as I exited the Methodist church,
it was waiting for me,
making the sky fizz like 7-Up
shooting across a frozen blue lake.
Each bubble was a thought
abandoned while I straightened my life
like a concerned god's spinal column
shifting in its precarious stack
of red hymnals, and I fainted straight
into my wife's strong arms.
As I swooned, I dreamed I was a tropical fish
in an aquarium somewhere in urban Ohio—
the store's owner enclosed behind his wall
of newspaper, like East Berlin, his cigar
smoldering at the cash register.

Then a skull-capped Jewish boy
slowly browsed the other fish,
and then stopped at my tank, thrilled
and scared. I bared my sharpest grin for him,
and let a bubble escape, dramatically,
from the aquarium of my mouth.
Watching it wobble to its death
in the air, the boy stared,
the boy stared.

ROBESPIERRE IS DEAD

We spent the day at the National Zoo
        weaving our way past the monkey house
            to where the elephant

bathed: he tossed a truck tire
        in the air like a toy.
            I sucked my snow cone too far

back and my white shirt
        drowned in purple and maybe
            a splash of elephant snot

from Jumbo who was then
        spraying his audience. I was
            fat as hell and imagining

a world without mirrors as I
        tucked it under my belt
            and flung on a spare

polo shirt from my gym bag
        and waddled to the penguins
            who could not grin but seemed

to be grinning anyway.
        In the reptile house you couldn't
            breathe so I dragged you out

choking into the sun, your hand
        strangling my left love handle
            and I thought everyone was worried

and confused, though on further
        reflection, I realized no one
                was watching us at all.

With a screech nearby
        an orange monkey mounted
                his wife and after three

thrusts jumped to his perch
        and fell asleep on a lump
                of his own excrement. Just about

that time, the hotdog stand opened,
        so I decided to get a 7-Up to soothe
                your sick stomach. As I was waiting

I noticed a young man with dirty
        black hair thrown over his eyes
                carving (with a sharpened spoon handle)

the phrase "Robespierre is dead" into
        a turnstile. "Probably," you said,
                "he killed him." As I looked back at the young man,

he was eating a snow cone near
        the prairie dog mound.
                How he smiled and crunched the ice

with his sharp purple teeth!

LOVING THE GOOD DRIVER

Those weekends we'd drive to Richmond—
alternating turns at the wheel or reading aloud
Teale's Autumn Across America
before our first baby when I could pause

and watch the pine wildness snap head-on
into angry patches of civilization,
watch cars from North Carolina
blur past, wonder

if the occupants had any boundaries,
or were mere luminaries if direction and velocity—
those weekends were the highway markers
signaling the hundredth, hundred-and-first

star expiring in the deep space
of our married life.
To what degree had we been?
Deeper

than a year at the knee, longer
than the whistle of Hurricane Unisex
that troubled the eastern seaboard
with its off-key tunes for more than a week,

and yet there we were in our new economy
car spraying over the rain-wet road
in the midst of the sudden sun, wishing somehow
our old age of travel were upon us,

watching a V of geese eaten
by a cloud with the face of Beethoven,
wishing we could live, nestled by trees,
in a renovated and climate enhanced
round barn with round furniture like thoughts

of a world stormed by peace or this peculiar
mixture of Virginia oxygen, hydrogen
and energy equaling page 311 times the speed
of sequel squared. We wanted to age gracefully,

modestly endowed, graciously endowed—whatever
it took—as we passed the cutoff to Cold Harbor—
as I zipped my jacket up—as you nibbled
an Oreo—as I sipped black tea

and then the sun rose on some darkened continent
in my head—as your suspicions of my delusions
of grandeur rolled off the windshield
on Midlothian Parkway—as I craved

a leg of mutton and a draught of mead.
What did I know?
I came to you because you were what I was
lonely for. And you took to marriage

the way a cat takes to drowning. Anyway
you were a good driver and I trusted you.
You also had a soothing reading voice. And when
we reached your sister's, she made some spicy ratatouille

and scrambled eggs. We shoveled it
down with toast, drank half-caff
and took a walk into the humid cold
to hear the bugs sing and watch the moon

rise like a Bismarck, jelly filled, we
beautifully childless, hormones shooting
through us like high octane fuel, the future
a string of Sunday evenings always feeling like the dregs

of a highly addictive extraction
even though the sky, clear
sparkling finales into the horizon,
hurtled so fast,
so long ago.

THE INVALID

Leaning my elbows
on the waist-high stucco wall
dividing sidewalk from beach,
I look at the empty white strand,
the afternoon sun glowing
over my left shoulder.
Behind me grows a tall birch,
its shade cast on the cool green
of the infirmary yard.

The sun warms my stiff joints and lungs
on this first day of spring.
The ocean is still cold. Everything seems
so far away. This illness sprang
up like a tree in the middle of my life;
in the midst of this sun,
soon it will recoil into a frond.
Soon it will be nothing but a pebble.
The sun, how warm,
and night, how far
away it is.

THE LAMP

In the dim light,
my face blossoms
from its electric motionlessness.
My slow turn loosens my hair.
Touching my thigh, the world blackens
for one leaf to fall
on a windless sphere of marble.

Dark rubbing on a coarse woven sheet:
who put me here
to always have just loved,
conscious in the warm river
flowing through the swallowing
darkness? Sometimes the seed
curls in its light-poor soil;
sometimes the sun cuts the blackness
to irradiate a silent life.

THE WOMAN IN THE WHITE PEUGEOT

Exactly. The car door slams, Peugeot, porcelain
and sleek as a fish. The woman, blond,
teeth like the car's enamel,

remembers the day her mind bent
at breakfast, the silverware glittering,
accusing her of thousands of murders,
her parents sitting at either end
of the table, their faces stark
like the faces of moths
magnified hundreds of times. Her senses,
now acute, feel the milk she swallows
at every stage, every valve of digestion,

steer and feel the wheels
touch nothing but skin. Blond hills
escape in the rearview mirror. The center-lines
pulse. Everything
is coherent now. Thoughts
line up like instructions on a bottle.

After the drugs, her body became important.
She could almost sense other creatures'
pain with it, the nerves
of her skin extended in waves.

She would lie on her bed, her eyes uncontrollable,
the lamp drifting, drifting, the living room
like a television with no vertical
hold. It took months before objects stopped
their distortion, lines of a calendar
snaking, even a lightswitch was a spineless
living jelly.

Twenty miles from town,
rain. The highway glosses over; red
taillights reflect like jet-flames on the pavement.
She turns on the radio: traffic situations
analyzed, updated.

THE ELECTRIC MOON

Drumming canyons of tall black air,
drinking somnambulists,
the Greyhound rumbles, stops, and so on
through farmtowns' milky lights.

In Albia, the electric moon flashes
pilsner ad: meteorites leaning
into luminous pastel blue, bleeding
threads of flame, white ice strobing
through yellow shot glasses, the tavern

door slapping under neon buzzing celestial.
One tired angel boards.
Toward daylight and Mt. Pleasant,
weather gears down into drizzle,

snaking ice water through greening hills.
The angel sleeps, wings smoothed under her
brown wool coat, head tilted toward
the window, the swimming
phonographic grooves, stubbled fields.

OPHELIA DROWNING

We grew up together, homely as storks,
stiffening our big knees against the cruelty of boys.
We danced with each other, palms touching
softly like those women in the Primavera—

their sweet circle of gazes. The fern-like branches
hovered over us through childhood. We became women,
beautiful, full of shadow.
One summer we came to the sea on a holiday.

Each day you swam out a bit
farther. At night we'd dry our glistening bodies
by the oven and eat fruit.
I remember sand drying on your legs

and arms, on your blue swim-suit
which reached up with its straps,
caressed you behind the neck and gently pulled
your head down to the thin white candle

and pile of orange peels (from which you picked
up a rind, squeezed it into the tear-
shaped flame). Orange oil shot into the candle
and lived its half-liquid moment

of explosion like a minor god expanding,
then collapsing into its own green body.
Your body became rounder
as if butter seeped into you

while you were sleeping, giving form
to your breasts and thighs.
If you had walked out of the bungalow then,
a man would have desired you,

and from his will, from his intestines
and lungs, he would have made
love to you, not even touching
you, blood being that dark and precise.

*

Out on the bleached sand I stood
one morning
as you went out further.
"Ophelia!" I cried,

but your ears were under, listening
to the steady wind of water.
Your belly
glistened blue like the underside of a dolphin.

Your death was serving its blow against me:
ears ringing, eyes filling
with liquid
sunlight,

as if I were drowning. These ten years,
in my mind, you never died, but came back,
heavy ankles lifting
out of water,

you falling
onto the beach, your hair caking sand,
your eyes staring at me, blank like a fish
gasping for its element.

Today, I'll imagine bending down,
putting my ear to your heart, my hand
over your mouth.
Perhaps tomorrow, it will be you

bowing your neck
to me, laughing,
your irises
filled with loose silt,

you digging your hand into my side
and toppling me onto the sand
and standing over me
as if you were a man, wanting inside.

THE CALLING

I stopped cleaning the black pots
in my kitchen because for once

in my lonely life I heard the night
singing as if each star had a voice.

Then I knew these were my brothers,
my angels, the crickets who watched

me get born so many years ago
in that black shanty made of old

peach crates and glue, where
mother died and dissolved like smoke

into the thin starlight.
I was raised by crickets, relying

on their black armor, until the stars were enough
to guide me, and then I followed

them, only to discover the brightness
of my flesh. And so it is tonight

that I tire of my vulnerable self
which has had no woman all these

years to weep around it, to make it
feel cruel and powerful. And so it is

I will never raise my head or act
surprised now that cold black night

has come to reclaim me, saying, "It is
enough brother, it is enough!"

PART THREE

THE BARBECUE

Time is some poor animal's flesh hissing over coals.
Someone pours a cold glass of wine.
Raises it to her lips. The color of pomegranate.
Life looks so smooth under these cedars.
Silhouettes in the smoke of spices.
The sun setting. A burning coin of silver.

In this park were once silver
mines. The lust for those coals
of metal. More precious than spices.
And thirsted for. More than wine.
The woman desires a long branch of cedar.
You want to give it to her. You want to watch its pomegranate

spits of resin fire. Its pomegranate
embers. She wears a necklace. Silver
angels and demons. You insert the cedar.
She stirs the coals.
More wine! she sings. And the priest brings more wine.
She rubs in an oil scented with spices.

But this isn't real. Forget the spices.
Forget all your notions of pomegranate.
Forget your forgetfulness in wine.
Forget your face in the lake-mirror's silver.
And let only your eyes glow. Like coals.
You no longer see the cedars.

You no longer smell the cedars.
And the intoxicating spices.
The woman you envisioned was merely coals.
Glowing in the heap. The thigh, a pomegranate
curvature this side of silver.
Warmed from the last few sips of wine.

The lake begins to color like wine.
In it, the reflection of a lone cedar.
The moon echoes silver.
In the air are the spices
of night. The heart is its own pomegranate.
The heart is a crumbling heap of coals.

WALKING WITH WILLIAM BLAKE UNDER THE TREES AT LAKE DARLING

The stars pierce the oak canopy like eyes
of angels I can't see; he can; a state
of lustrous vision he'd burn in me: the cries
of heaven from mouths bejewelled with stars. I wait

for his ignition to my spirit eye, hope
to ease in pools of hydrochloric phrase, possessed
by the verse that once embalmed me, scope
the landscape of the muse like an alien, at least.

Down by the lake, preteens smoke crack, despising
their angry and littered heaven, and Bill sings, "This state
called Beulah, a pleasant lovely shadow arising
where no dispute can come," and I think, "That's just great,

Bill," as midnight's dry brain pops and crackles to flame,
and one angel on the beach screams God's name.

TRYING TO SURVIVE DEATH'S LITTLE WEATHER

The flesh of clouds.
       The closed eyelid
              of horizon.

The water's restless
       sleeping body
              pulling a wave

over its shoulder
       like a sheet.
              The hair of morning

purple and black.
       The creaking boats.
              The motors winding

to sea.
       The propped window
              of the bedroom

crashing shut.
       Nothing, necessarily, asks
              to breathe

or be touched.
       Morning comes
              as a table

and the shadow
       of a cup.

I HAVE A NEW BRAIN

Green flash, setting sun: it's the blood
subtler than blood: it's in everything.

The dog next door howls, "Oh, I am so lonely!"
In the oatmeal tree the cardinal sings,

"Finito! Finito!" And I believe.
I look into the mirror: two faces: neither of them are me.

One: the face of the body that belongs
to soil. One: the face of man

in green light belonging to the sun,
its setting. On the other hand,

the meandering of smoke
searching out the draft

in the window-- always considering the exit
as a thing of beauty, considering

the wind, its making, its act, its result,
its metaphor of being itself.

Outside a child says, "Hi," and the guilty
man passing says, "What's that?"

Your friend is having trouble comprehending
this evening. I have a new brain.

Its name is Leroy. It's got a bunch
of land round New Salem, good fertile land.

Its boys' names are Bear, Animal, and Gunk.
They live in the woods, but they've accomplished

a passionate ballet. When the shotgun fires,
there is a blooming into the night.

Purdy, says the boys. Fourth
of July, and there's plenty

of beer and shells. Purdy like a possum
is purdy when his eyes lock glowing

on oncoming lights. That's all ye need to know.

NOTEBOOK

The thin blue lines
upon which the words
perch-- each letter
a bird on a power line.
Feed them. Spread
the sunflower and cracked
corn and millet upon
the ground. Watch
each letter be called
to you by hunger.
Hear their undisciplined
singing.
Be lost, and if you
drop bread crumbs
as you fall into the
darkness of the tall trees,
watch them be consumed
by such scarlet measures
and intervals of blue.

THE ANGEL

The specter of a man keeps reappearing
in the doorway. He's all cartilage, an operation
of musculature, no skin, no blood fast
in the veins. Some would call him a phantom;
others, an accumulation of hungers
as old as fire, visible when the god begins

to peel the head back like an orange, begins
to monkey with the perceptions, to reappear
in his sinewy angel, and sing like no hunger.
Once, in the hospital after an operation
that dried the soul to paper, the body phantom
approached the foot of the bed, as the faucet

dripped out the seconds, as the black faucet
of his open mouth issued a white noise which began
far up the Mississippi in the phantom
rustle of yellow leaves. Then reappearing
on the north wall, a sunlight opera
of numbers in tens, twenties, thirties... hungers

that knew all the years and obsessions, hungers
that defined the boundaries of what I fought
to keep: a body, a few coins, this operation
of penning for no one's ears, this beginning
of middles aflame and ends charred, and he reappearing
now, the membrane of his wings a phantom

translucence, as I am alone, today, home with the phantom
of what I can't control. The syringe hungers
for a new landing pad of flesh; it's reappearing
now in the form of the angel, ugly with the fast
starkness of the world beyond himself. He begins
to tell me who he really is, an operation

he ceases mid-sentence. But I know he's the operative
of the ruins of heaven. He is the phantom
agent with nothing left to report. He begins
to tell me he was just like me once, a hunger
too quick to extinguish itself, a ceaseless faucet
of habits and repetitions and wounds reappearing.

But now he understands: an operative, a phantom,
a hunger, a beginning, a faucet,
a fountain reappearing. Now he knows.

THE DES MOINES RISING AT BENTONSPORT

River, quarter mile wide here, brown
as motor oil. Currents swirl an Amoco cup,
suck it down (fifty-three miles up
from the Miss) near a clinically dead town.

Foam dots the ripples like globs of spit
below the maples. Cottonwoods skirt the bank
as if calling the other side for thanks
or help. And orange in the leaves, orioles perhaps; it's

a difficult song, full of the confluence
of failure and rotten luck and grace
like undertow shadowed by the crusted iron

crisscross of a bridge. And brown moths dance
on the childish weeds of the bank, a face
on each wing, and water inches in like prairie fire.

TEACHER

—To David Wojahn

Your words were conscience to me: Keats singing
how delicately time flowers
to accomplish the impossible: the songs
of spring budded in the future.

I worked ambition,
curving its bony fingers
around the curse:
meditating a single icy bloom.

If it was all failure, perhaps you knew
it would be: verses reincarnating,
opening like violets
in a graveyard, without violence,

without breath. This is all I have
to pay you:
their subtle fragrance,
their half-remembered blend of red and blue.

FROM THEIR ORBIT IN THE HIGH DARK

O fragment. O equation. O decimal. My dear Deus Ex Machina,

The first Assignment, some sustained exercise
in division: 1984--the fabled year

of surveillance cameras behind every mirror
and satellites so perfect

they could from their orbit in the high dark
read any manuscript before its ink was dry: bullets

of memory divided by the trick, divided by shelves
of books corridoring back to the dimly lit

desk the color of sand and early boundaries of dream: fiction
merely a form

of counterintelligence and sub-division
as when I was camping and the morning illumination

revealed gold clad extraterrestrials, twenty of them, divided
        by the clearing
in the mist: back then I thought a story was

an infernal fraction tempered and valved
to resemble, at times, music: vapors rose

from the creek, I was staggered by the clarity
of their armor, like millions of polished rays

divided by the color of luxury and the day you came down
from Baltimore, and Mrs. Ex Machina, to review (i.e. dismantle)

the short stories I'd sent: I had ignored
the signs, the warnings: "don't drink" and the torso

of polished gold overlay
frozen in the refrigerated air near the ladies' room

in the I.M. Pei wing of the National Gallery:
my head was swirling with the wounded

flutter of dogwood trees, blankets of ivy
like lives tortured to California and then baptized

by the Pacific's blue verisimilitude: we met
at the cafe in the tunnel between

the two gallery buildings, a place
bright with tourists, reproductions like raw steak,

fountains of snow and mountain rain: memory,
it turned out, was the assignment,

that tremble in my walk
as I ascended the crescent moon:

as you bought one of those funky sandwiches made from a croissant,
and a beer whose name I misread

as "Old Armistice"
and I ordered a fish

from the Sumerian because I felt
biblical and wanted to cubit forever:

my consciousness
of rattlesnakes under tree stumps blue with moss,

cool boulders, conglomerate and sparkling with flecks of mica,
compelled me, and soon it was there: as you said

my stories needed less
throat clearing and should begin

with heavy chords like a "kick-ass" rock band:
the valley smoking red and lavender,

the trembling towns twinkling as night came on:
"You should make your stories

like that sculpture of Jean Arp's
at the end of the tunnel."

From every angle
it looked like a woman's torso

in the delectable metallic flames
of thrust and revision: that last spear

of sunlight threatening the east,
vanquished at last by its own westward impetus:

the anti-elegy merely dreamed
at the end of ten years,

Mrs. Ex Machina gone, just, and I can't imagine it:
what I've come to see, winging in the middle

of nothing: blond hair chopped like a cutting remark,
like a flapper with a .38 packed

in a black sequined purse:
invisible now in the dusk: her fiction?--

outlawed angel's wine: calling to its mate:
lifting its vision to the cold stars,

to the sculptor of the mountains and fields:
giving sporting notice to its prey: forgive me,

Deus. It's one of those nights
it's snowing and I'm alone

and I'm a little bit crazy
and more than a little drunk: sensing

you: I refuse to weep and say
I wish I had 1/10th of anything: alone:

and yet she could praise and curse
and make the whole fragmented world drop

sparkling from her tongue.

DEAR ROGER

Ice appears to ooze down the steps
like maple syrup and I slip and nearly
crack my prize coconut on the lumber
to the lush ferned office of your smiling black beard.

Cardinals stick out their tongues and warble
and I'm standing at the front door now
feeling how stiffly it's locked
and admiring with some dread

the delicate rosettes
crafted near each corner of the door's
window a hundred years ago or more
by a mildly retarded gentleman

named Clem Beesleman, now buried
in Montpelier's Lady of the Protective
Undergarments cemetery and miniature
golf course. I can see you

sinking one among the tombstones as I stand
jiggling the doorknob, see you in double
reverse upside-down through infinity
in the door's handsome beveled leaded window

swirling in some places with nearly transparent
rainbow flaws and bubbles as I scream
"Professor, tell me, what is poetry?"
Your reflection drops its putter

in mid-stroke upon the headache-like monument
of Edna Cravitz Hungarian Cheesefamine Ross,
dead March 30th, 1896 in ankle-deep snow
with a decanter of pomade in one hand

and a Faberge Easter egg in the other
and you shout your granite chipping anapests:
"Get your tuchas off my porch and
damn you to southern fried stanzas

of geese disemboweled with Ginsu
pocket assault blades, $9.95 plus
handling and shipping, in the bovine
humor of your checking account

which spread its gracious cloak
before your feet to enter the Gopher
Gulch MFA in Creative Writing Program
(low residency format) to tread softly,

if you tread on my dreams, with a penchant
for spilling Vermont ale and molten medallions
of aged cheddar on my doormat's freshly cleansed,
and blessed by a well oiled hatha yoga master,

nap and saffron 'Welcome.' Be gone with thee!"
The frozen snail in the parlor window
easily curls in its deathlike shell
and keeps the carcasses of flies in stitches,

so to speak, since there's nothing funny
as I turn to greet your voice trailing
from the putting green, frozen and glittering,
as you sink one in a freshly dug

six-foot-under rectangle of finality
and rejoice, "A birdie! By all that
is sacred on the hoary breast of Moses!"
and fling the metal claw of your success

at a huge black and winged creature
perched on the white branches of an elm
casting its spell over the icy pit,
a whisper in telepathic entreaty:

"Does this mean a job is utterly out of the question?"

Yours, prostrate,

Rocket J. Squirrel, M.F.A.

THE EMPEROR'S TAPESTRY

He tasted no languages on his tongue,
    just sand.
            He had a certain amount of hopelessness

hanging over his eyes
    like a tapestry of white roses.
            He slept, and dreaming created

cities of echoing clay.
    He listened well, he didn't ask questions,
            he beheaded his teachers.

He had a few desperate books he was reading,
    a few wine-stained poems–
            the swan's icy fluting could rise

in his window like the sun.
    He knew when new birds stirred the pond
            to live, to eat,

or merely ignite the water and fly on.

THE PHILOSOPHER SAVANT CONTEMPLATES
A SUMMER EVENING

Breathing aloud, O death, in pure illumination
As Whitman casting no shadow, the garden
Rippling as if he were endless within
Lit on each color, each flower that's been

Despite this awareness, my focus now
On some destiny marred. But it's curious
The jagged detail of eclipse, shadow
So shifted with its world of breezes

And illumination—each leaf, each flight
Flitting under the shadow of the fig.
I pictured a group of blackbirds, a night
Looking at the garden, a green-blue streak

Of sky. The orange-roofed house, the boil
Of potato soup, taste of olive oil.

SEASCAPE AT SAINTES-MARIES-DE-LA-MER
after Van Gogh

Colors of the Mediterranean—
changeable as moods or seasons.
Green to violet— outcroppings
of sharpened stone; blue to pink— waves
dissolving onto canvas, body atomized
into spectrum of sunrise.

And Theo, there are sailboats!
I should write you:
these thoughts change to wind
just as the lone fisherman sails
from the stern— rudder cutting
the sliding sea.
                              The vision
assumed in these paintings:
crescendo of waves: chaos
frozen
               as I stroke the dream
of walking jagged waters,
to grasp the salted gunwales,
the drenched sails, to speak to him—
the grey tiller still in his callused hands—

as I would speak to myself,
argue the hundred variations of citron
lighting the roofs of Arles—
                                    but his rejoinder
is not a voice— I don't know what it is— nothing
more than an intimation of storm,

maybe, something I imagined
resolved with a brisk stroke of cobalt—
                    But
paint is the hunting water
for irresolution--
see it when I rest my vision
from a long day's work--
a hue-shifting sea on which all longings
drift for land--
a citron coast from where longings sail
stark green bottles toward Africa.

THE NEW PAINTING

Turning to her lover, the painter of wishes, she says,
"You know what I wish?"
and then
stops short, because she doesn't know.
The trombone duet of a crossing train
slides over the scene:
the lake water, her tall lover,
their ladder leaned against the cherry tree.
She only knows she wishes. It's like
trying to say I want to go home
in a language that has no words for it.
To tell the truth, she and her friend stopped at this lake-
side park for the view, to watch the wind
dimple the water like a child blowing
on a spoon,
because, for so long, there had been virtually no sky in her world.
She can't help now but drop her lover's two names
into the lake like sugary dice
in the sun's coffee.
She wonders, "Should I feel strengthened by this?"
When they stood under the firs
near the shore, he motioned to her.
The sun-yellowed grasses pounced
just where the lane disappeared
into the cobalt trees and the soft fish-white
underbelly of narrative.
"He's watching," he said to her, "that detective
in the grungy stationwagon." And she looked
far away and said, "What?!"
A thermos cup of coffee, a cup born
full of dark ideas that captured her unaware

just as the orange light
above the tousled bed earlier this morning
captured her attention as she rested dreaming
that warm replenishing fluid.
Yet, she is chilled at the idea of being caught,
her husband traveling and yet watching her
through this other.
"It was inevitable," she says. She thinks, "So the naked
reflect what colors flame at them,
as if interiors were meant to digest
one whole, soul and all, like hell.
So this is what little rooms dream
when they fall asleep."
Once, sitting on a bench on the mall in D.C.,
she overheard one congressional wife
advising the other, "There's only one thing
you can do!" (she wanted to call the relationship
two worlds
singing to be parted by the proximity
of a bowl aflame with tangerines)--
"Divorce him! Before he divorces you!" she said,
and the other wife said, "What?!"
positively chilled and delighted.
Later that day her lover continues to paint her image.
She notices the nudes
have grown larger. Someday, she thinks,
it will be the detail of a thigh alone
purpled by the blanket of the day bed.
She imagines the squeal of a train
in her blood
snaking on the light
blues and oranges, the sweet bathroom tiles
of the damned.

She turns to her painter and says,
"You know what I wish? Sometimes, like today,
the sun rises and gives birth
to the gentle summer greens,
floods the vegetables
with the searing whiteness
of eggshells."
"Sometimes," she continues as her painter swirls a nipple, blue, brown, pink,
"sometimes I know exactly what I mean
by 'home.'"

AN ORDINARY DRINKING GLASS

I pour more beer
and the darkness dies
in the amber fingers
of light.

On TV, the cartoon dog dives
into--not a tub of water,
not a bucket of water, but--
an ordinary drinking glass!

Flourish!

Splash!

He is compressed below the rim--
a sponge dog
with red striped swim
suit blurring as the trap door opens
and the pig in the blue jacket, red bow tie,
and no pants (like a bad dream--no
genitals either) waves bye-bye.

When I was twenty-three
I worked as a typist in the Library
of Congress. Every morning
I would take my urge to sleep
and my wife
who also worked on the Hill
to the red line
and board the local
to Union Station.

74

I would watch carefully out the window
thinking
my beauty didn't care much for me
for she had a book
into which she sank as one would sink into a forest
of stone buddhas hushed
with poisonous vines.

The train flowed, snakelike, and above ground
the best of trees I caught
were similar to the light
that seduces you as general anesthesia takes hold.

Daytime, after work, from our window I could see straight
into the apartment
where an elderly man lay bedridden.
I imagine he would lie all day with his mouth
open, and, if his eyes were alive,
staring back at our apartment, just as austere but for a few
geranium leaves sprouting in old mayonnaise
jars of water on the few shelves
we owned like sticks and sand.

Somehow, he reminded me that, as a child, alone,
I turned on the television for companionship.
And it was one of those fantastic
gardens in which irises and roses
bloom in an instant--silent explosion
of petals into a joyous brightness and giving
till that unavoidable turn.

Imagine loud cracks of thunder.
Imagine being pulled out slowly by the current
of the sea, by the tide, by radio
signals, a violin played in a lonely
cabin on an island off Labrador.
Imagine the yellow-lit windowpanes.
Imagine the night
black as soy sauce.

Our cartons of Chinese food
sat on the card table we called home.
And the classical radio station
kept us in tune
with the big city
of perfection
no man bothered to create.

At night, from our window,
I could see taxis bringing the people home--lovers
who sparkled from dances above the river;
others who wore loneliness like a damp gray wool;
and the little white-haired one
who would sooner have her throat opened
in a parking lot
than be stripped of her purse weighing less
than fifty-five dollars
and a scream.

I rinsed my razor-bloodied face in the sink
and ran the back of my hand over my chin.

My wife's name was whispered
by the rumpled linen.

I saw the light dying
in the amber fingers
of darkness.

I poured my name
easily
into an ordinary glass.

PART FOUR

He said
To go smash me
On the rocks
Of my self
And when I showed him
He was p-pleased

THE WINE-DARK HOUSE

In the wine-dark house
I wade and read
Odysseus fording jealousy
and light. The bleeding heart
attacks have not yet bloomed
on their cactuses.
We have punched our tickets
to the kingdom of silence tonight.
In the wine-dark house
the claws of the love seat
have not rended me.
And the lamp is like pale hair.
Blessed are the seven candlesticks
that guide my ways to and from there.
Outside, the crocuses penetrate
the basketball court.
There is a planter of impatiens
whistling in the hoop. But in the wine-dark
he does not hear me
reading late, and she sleeps
with her reading hand
ironed between her thighs.
This is the night of profound questions.
This is the night of missed directions.
I feel the hand of the cold dead muse
on my shoulder. This is Liberty Valance.
The blue eye of the living room collapses
to a pin of guilty light.

And in the wine-dark night
my pages ruffle like a hand full
of avian white. I have taken
my lessons in patience
from the wine-dark house.
There's an oracle
in the door ajar.
In the wine-dark house
the wine that has been poured
is darkness, you see?
I drink the wine
and the wine drinks me.

FATHER

I.

My father is justice; in dreams always
ruling in my favor, rapping gavel,
hugging me close, defying distance.
From a library comes father. The books
tattered, brown, ancient as saint's relics.
I take two thin volumes with me as I go.

The train steps into motion over rails
and fist-sized cinders. Piles of leaves burn filled
with green and amber. Under the earth, hands
rise stained with crosses and smoke and silver.
The traffic on Rhode Island Avenue
moves orderly without a single choice.

My father steps onto his porch. In November, a blue
sky wakes like one eye out of darkness;
the presidential motorcade looms
wreathed with black orchids. Back in the Midwest
is a broken window; my father sees
wildflowers growing in an old black tire.

II.

I imagine, somewhere, a man sitting
in a dark observatory; crickets
in the unobserved night grasses, singing.

And he is God, in the image of my
father, who from a star is staring down
on the ever-shifting constellation

of souls on earth. He saw Edison put
electric lamps in country houses. Yes.
He's glad for our desire to have more light.

He's glad for our desire; and when he
alone is satisfied, he takes a road
much like the empty road we want to take.

Few things have reassured him like the sound
of a working clock: the sound with empty
boxes in front of it and full boxes
behind. In an empty kitchen, where
someone has kneaded, the sound's loose snowfall settles
over linen-covered bowls, and at a
window overlooking bricks and mosses,
holds up empty hands of baptism.

III.
Under the lamps of autumn nights,
my father reads "Macbeth" and I "King Lear."
The library: Shakespeare--
Elizabethan roof of steep green tiles--
a portrait of the man in edifice.

In the library is broken glass,
a window shattered like a spider's web,
and through a hole I see the twilight air,
and next to Shakespeare other thoughts appear,

at a great distance. The train lurches forward;
the station with its circling moths it shed;
the lights of small towns float away like buoys;

motion is in all of us. Shakespeare's
broken glass we stand behind, myself,
you father, and justice with his pale-blue
mind, and something I haven't mentioned yet,
the "Skater's Waltz" and how in dreams it plays
always when people are in motion. It
still plays, and then fades with consciousness--
spinning dying spins as a skater spins
becoming an umbrella of motion.

1969

Mother spreads fudge out in a pan,
without a ripple, the way
the Florentine painters disguised brush marks,
through crafted subtlety.

I pick up the cat named Monet
and search through her orange, brown
and white fur for cockle-burrs,
prickly seeds that seem to have
a mind of their own.

At 40, Mother is pregnant
with my youngest brother.
I am 10 years old. The philodendrons
lounge in the sunlight on top of the TV set;
the orange paint of the living room
drones with summer.

*

My father is at his television shop in the country.
He works under fluorescent light, blue smoke
of the soldering gun drifts to the ceiling.
He fingers the schematic like a page of the bible,
wetting his fingertips as he turns a page, glancing
through the lower lenses of his bifocals.
He has been doing this for twenty years,
and has been through every change in technology
as if he has lived through lives. The green mouth
of the oscilloscope flickers as the needlelike probe

touches soldering joints of resistors and capacitors.
All the guts of the television are cleaned and sparkling
like candy: resistors, brown cylinders marked with fruit stripes;
and capacitors, glossy as chocolate covered caramels.
Now the technicians are out on their calls,
and the shop is quiet, you can hear my father breathe
softy, absorbed in his circuitry.

*

My sister is on the edge of either leaving or staying home.
In two years she will be living in Canada,
but we will not know. She will take the first
of a hundred acid trips,
and, in subsequent years, give
me presents: a ceramic jar of natural herb tea
(which looks suspicious, so I never try any); a light-blue
shirt embroidered with pyramids and hurricanes; and last,
a porcelain tea set brushed with the calligraphy of brown grass.

*

My older brother lives with his wife in a trailer
in Ames, Iowa. My mother always rings her hands
and stares out the north window during tornado warnings.
They are the current hope for grandchildren, but the first
will not be born for five years. We visit them every
other weekend. Their place is the blandness of newly
married couples--too new to have gained any character,
and there is never anything interesting to eat. Their
gravy lacks salt, their chicken is underdone, and their
television is snowy. She shows me a collection of bees
and wasps, says she got an "A" on the project.

86

The best thing they do for me is take me on a bike ride
to a stagnant pond. Knee-deep in mud, I look
to a lavender sky, blackbirds in a bone-white tree,
and frogs by the thousands, each
as big as a child's face.

BOTH HALVES TOGETHER

Like the man who says, "It's my invention;
it came to me while I was on the john!"
I know exactly what to do with my life:

One half will repair the spines of dwarves,
so they will stand corrected; the other half
will get to know our feathered friends better,

like a bitter colony of lice, will sit
in golden kinship as autumn smoke rises
from the leaves, will chew on a piece of

celery and feel how good its stringy wateriness
tastes in the open air. Both halves together
will wish they had gotten into real estate

early on, but mostly they will admire
those who spent their lives serving humanity,
those who rescued children from the jaws of mice,

those who poisoned the silver-skinned men
from Pluto with orange juice, those who are
tucked away in the ground with a few

roses on top of them, and a few sweet words
cut into the sadness.

NIGHT AND SPINACH

Night and spinach is boiling
in the dangerous pan
that likes to char and make
my food taste like a cross-
beam of a shoe factory
after the fall of Richmond.

The Great E-masturbator,
as fifth grade boys
at Lincoln Elementary
like to call him,
swings his gawky shoes
onto the desk of Jefferson
Davis, who is through
being president of the
Confederate States of
America and is fleeing
in women's clothes
through the Southern swamps.

This all happens as I cook
supper. The paper snow-
flakes are on the window.
I can barely see the swing-
set and the bird feeder.
The night is playing
with the gliding horse
like an anemic child
or like a bleeder.
Imagine night, a hemophiliac
perforating its skin

on lightning rods and church
steeples, its wounds
above us, its white sparkling
blood. The night dies
as a child. It's such
a simple and needful thing
to cook food for my little
ones; a union corporal
by the James River leans
into his campfire to retrieve
the boiling coffee and scorching
beans; someone plays a guitar
softly; the music is coming
from that black curtain
of trees, from those
hemorrhaging lights.

AT THE BREAK OF DAY ON MY WOODEN PORCH

The pigeons have all flown in now, and I
have messages from all over. Here's one
from Walt Whitman; he says everything

is fine in D.C.; the troops are having
their arms sawn off and yet he stays
there and reads them letters and generally

livens the drab little place up. James Joyce
is in Paris at Shakespeare and Co.
rushing the publication of that monster

book, Ulysses. Homer is blind as usual.
Thoreau goes for walks every day
straight through birds' nests, thorns and ponds

and never manages to lose a toe
to a snapping turtle. And myself at
thirteen has sent me a message

from a summer many years ago. He
is enjoying California, though
his baby brother vomited in the car

while on the road to Needles, where the tall
thin rocks thrust into the air. And I wonder
how much blue sky I can take in now

and save for later? And will that ladder
rot, leaning on the eaves? And how many times
will I have to dig leaves out of the rainspout,

or keep the pigeons from crying
in their cages at night? Here's a message
from Emily Dickinson who eyes

the blackbird eating an earthworm,
and nobody buys it for a minute,
not, at least, while she lives. And then

she reincarnates and is Robert Frost,
and is rewarded and cursed forever
to be remembered as a great poet

who neglected, almost to a criminal
degree, his family. And of course
there's Dylan Thomas, who I think was

so embarrassed by his own behavior
he had to go ahead and kill himself
with drink. Do not go gentle, because if

you when gently nobody would
make a big fuss over you. Be lofty,
brave, pompous, out of keeping

with the times, and you will be remembered
ten times over. But oh, who, may I ask,
really wants to be remembered if all

we're doing is riding this gigantic sperm
cell out into the stars?

IMPROBABILITY'S BEST FRIEND, REJECTION

Rejection sits in the far corner of a library, reading
A forty year old magazine.
He says to himself, "Here I am, so far in Life."
And people look at the buttons on
His shirt and say to themselves,
"Those are his buttons, that is
At least one way we can tell
Who he is."

Rejection had a friend, Improbability, who shaved his
Eyebrows (in an effort to be less than average,
Or more—it depends on how you
Look at it).
Rejection ate only raw white cabbage for each
Meal. Rejection's imagination tells
Him he looks like a cabbage,
A transformed fairy tale creature,
Alive by virtue of repeating the story
Each time before bed.

It's not good to be alone.
He can't touch other people
Because he isn't one. Rejection says,
"God has my paramour out there,
I know. I'll find her when I've learned
To be 100%. She wears a necklace
Of wild carrot flowers. She's
Known several men before now, but she
Is so much like myself she shyly
Creeps to the mirror each morning and allows
A shoulder's width space to stand near the vowels
Of her breasts."

Each morning, Rejection washes his face in a basin of warm water.
There is no life but rest;
The day glows and then falters
Through closed curtains.
He shuts his eyes and answers Acceptance's salutation.
He says to the subtle face: "Tell
Me my fortunate friend... I'll someday return
The favor... and give you a life of your own."

VIVA LA SESTINA

The ethereal powers (they) say Elvis has reincarnated
at the zoo. You'll see a rare lyre bird married
to the color of its plumage. That is he. One falcon
with an eye on it all won't matter. Her breakfast
is a mouse, not music. And Elvis's story
konked out around a half-eaten cheeseburger. End of character.

Today the ethereal powers are out of character.
The gods of ancient Greece have reincarnated
into living men and women on the streets of Des Moines. Each story
unsatisfactory and heroic (i.e. tragic) and married
to some apocalypse. This morning after a breakfast
of cold salmon and coffee, I saw the falcon

perched on a light pole. It was a cute falcon.
How can a raptor be so small? I thought. How out of character.
I could see the zoo from my breakfast
window; I could see the reincarnated
sun levitate above the cages, the sun married
to the shadows with which it danced. Its story

was a simple one. As Elvis sang, I found a story
that suddenly made perfect sense. A Ford Falcon
with a bad muffler smoked in the street. My married
friends think I'm nuts—how I character
my conversations with the mythical Elvis, a reincarnation
of rhinestone and a breakfast

of valium, Pucker schnapps, champagne, and the Breakfast
of Champions. For example, here's an odd and little-known known story.
In Las Vegas, Elvis knew this guy who was the reincarnation
of Kubla Khan. He sat on a sandalwood throne with a falcon
taloned on his shoulder. This character
would marry

you to anything you wanted. Elvis wanted to be married
to his Cadillac and his gun. The falcon,
blinded by his leather hood, ruffled his feathers. The Khan character
performed a fire ceremony. End of story.
I don't know what you had for breakfast
buddy. I had the cold sacrament and the King reincarnated.

A USEFUL MEMBER OF SOCIETY

Forlorn as a '57 Philco
the way I felt filing schematics
by date and model number, each print

featuring a black-and-white mugshot on the cover,
the RCA's looking bourgeois and uppity,
the Philco's looking plywood and metal

and working class: maybe a grille of tweed
to dress things up, never cherry wood
cabinetry like the Radio Corporation of America

whose theater-like cathedrals
shrined Kukla, Fran and Ollie
in sculpted mahogany.

Philco's looked like they belonged to dime novel
detectives
or suicides.

I would sit on a wooden stool at a row
of dinged up green file cabinets that once belonged
to Sam Spade or Uncle Sam, and shuffle these strange

maps which showed the way electricity
should flow and be trapped and sedated
into a useful member of society. At 5:30

Walter Cronkite appeared on 16
simultaneous screens to tell us the score
in Belfast. There was the humming of raw

electrical frustration all over the shop.
Wires hung from rafters, oscilloscopes
fluttered their green sine wave mouths,

there was the crackling of charges
enlivening the Frankenstein's monsters
of TV chassis balanced on nicked tables

and metal carts and makeshift hoists.
Gus Kilmer operated on his chassis
with the arrogance of a bad surgeon

obligated to the survival of the patient,
but not wholeheartedly. You could see
the gleam of a ball-peen hammer in Gus's eyes,

an instinctive abandonment
to destruction. Once a power transformer
sparked into a nasty tarrish flame

because of Gus's short attention span,
and Mr. Retention, owner of the shop,
stumbled upon the unattended conflagration

and electrical stench, screaming threats
of firing Gus's ass and docking
his severance check. Gus's eyes welled

up like a baby's. Retention had
a soft spot for contrite nincompoops.
They changed the damned transformer

under a rain of cussing. And son-of-a-bitch
if the reassembled set didn't work fine.
Just a slight smell of the burn.

*

Some days rain. And after, the windows
to be squeegeed.
There'd always be a swallow's

nest of dead birds,
a halo of wasps.
I didn't mind this was my life.

I didn't know it could or should be anything
than it was. And so I'd snap
the lid off a sweating Pepsi

and drink to the day's end
not claiming I was different than anybody
else who owned a '69 Catalina

with 8 track and air-con and a sunset
to urge me home
to a room whose constant salutation

flickered in the dial
of a radio catching music
from far off Denver and the frying

pops and static of millions
of crying galaxies. Amen. This
was nobody's life but my own.

SIGN OF THE TIMES

Saw Roger the other day--I was driving
west, his retard shuttle east.
The sunlight struck his face.

I saw that same hopeless look--I could tell
he had been punished for stealing
peanut butter or eating instant coffee

from the bulk bin or peeing in the sink
or sucking on his bar of deodorant soap.
Poor Roger. I remember how he signed

"bowel movement" anytime he wanted
to describe a transaction with money--payment,
spend.   I once took walks down

the gravel path of Mentally Disabled Central
to the Physically Challenged Cemetery just to watch
him smoke his ration of generic full tar

kings. Bowel movement he would sign
asking if I had any money to buy
him a Mountain Dew. Bowel movement

I would sign back to indicate
no spare change. We would stand
at Highway One at the gates of the Sympathy

Challenged World and sign bowel movement
as a greeting to the cars speeding
to Eldon or Fairfield or Mount Pleasant.

"You know, Roger," I'd say, sheltered
under the wings of the stone angel,
"this life is sometimes so..."

and I would pause to sign silently.
"Mmmm...Mmmmm,"
Roger would nod in agreement,

awkwardly lighting another cigarette;
bowel movement, emphatic.
I don't know; it always seemed to be fall

or spring, fall or spring, always some mud
on the ground, and at five o'clock
I would get in my car and drive home

to another dinner of rocks and gravy
on toast. "Goodbye Roger," I would say
as along side the car he jogged

signing.

ABOUT THE AUTHOR

Rustin Larson's poetry has appeared in *The New Yorker, The Iowa Review, North American Review, Poetry East, The Atlanta Review* and other magazines. His collection *Crazy Star* was selected for the Loess Hills Book's Poetry Series in 2005. Larson won 1st Editor's Prize from *Rhino* magazine in 2000 and has won prizes for his poetry from The National Poet Hunt and The Chester H. Jones Foundation among others.

A five-time Pushcart nominee, and graduate of the Vermont College MFA in Writing program, Larson was an Iowa Poet at The Des Moines National Poetry Festival in 2002 and 2004, a featured writer in the DMACC Celebration of the Literary Arts in 2007, 2008, and has been highlighted on the public radio programs *Live from Prairie Lights* and *Voices from the Prairie*. He is the host of the radio talk show *Irving Toast, Poetry Ghost* (http://www.kruufm.com) and lives in Fairfield, Iowa.

www.ingramcontent.com/pod-product-compliance
Lightning Source LLC
Chambersburg PA
CBHW032018090426
42741CB00006B/650

* 9 7 8 1 4 2 1 8 9 0 7 7 7 *